The Economic Atlas:

Mapping the World's Financial Landscape

By

Iram Nazir

SHORT SUMMARY:

"The Economic Atlas: Mapping the World's Financial Landscape" is a book that aims to provide a comprehensive overview of the world economy and the financial landscape. The book covers basic concepts and terms used in the world economy, the financial markets and instruments, the impact of globalization, the current state of the world economy, managing financial risk, and potential future economic trends. The book is intended to be informative and engaging, and encourages readers to continue learning about the complexities of the world economy.

Introduction:

Overview of the book's purpose and goals:

"The Economic Atlas: Mapping the World's Financial Landscape" is a book that aims to provide readers with a comprehensive understanding of the world economy and financial landscape. Through the book's exploration of fundamental concepts and terms, financial instruments and markets, and the complexities of globalization, readers will gain a deeper understanding of the impact that these factors have on the global economy.

The purpose of "The Economic Atlas" is to offer a comprehensive and accessible resource for individuals, businesses, and policymakers who seek to understand the complexities of the world economy. The book aims to provide readers with the knowledge and insights necessary to navigate the modern financial landscape, make informed decisions about investments, and manage financial risk.

Explanation of the importance of understanding the world economy and financial landscape:

In today's interconnected world, the global economy has a significant impact on individuals, businesses, and governments. Therefore, it is essential to understand the fundamental concepts and terms that drive the world economy and financial markets, and how they interrelate. Understanding the complexities of globalization, financial markets, and the world economy can help individuals and businesses make informed decisions about their financial future, mitigate risk, and navigate the challenges of a dynamic global economy.

"The Economic Atlas" offers readers a unique opportunity to gain a deeper understanding of the world economy and financial landscape. The book is an essential resource for individuals seeking to make informed decisions about their finances, businesses looking to succeed in a global market, and policymakers working to address the economic challenges of the modern world

Chapter 1: The Fundamentals of the World Economy

Part 1: Basic Concepts and Terms Used in the World Economy

Understanding the basic concepts and terms used in the world economy is crucial to making informed decisions about personal and business finances, investing, and economic policy. This chapter will provide a detailed overview of the essential concepts and terms used in the world economy, including definitions and explanations of key economic indicators, such as GDP, inflation, and unemployment.

Gross Domestic Product (GDP) is one of the most important economic indicators and measures the total value of all goods and services produced within a country's borders during a specific period, typically a year. Understanding how GDP is calculated and its significance in the world economy is crucial for policymakers, investors, and businesses seeking to gain insights into the overall economic health of a country.

Inflation is another essential economic concept, and measures the rate at which the prices of goods and services rise over time.

Understanding inflation is crucial for businesses and individuals seeking to make informed decisions about pricing and investments, as well as for policymakers who must ensure price stability within their economies.

Unemployment is a measure of the percentage of the total workforce that is without employment but actively seeking work. High levels of unemployment can be a significant economic challenge, as they can lead to lower economic growth and increased social unrest. Understanding the factors that contribute to unemployment and the policies that can mitigate it is critical for policymakers and individuals seeking to make informed decisions about employment opportunities.

Part 2: The Economic System and Its Various Components

The world economy is made up of a complex system of interrelated components, each with its unique role and function. This chapter will provide a detailed overview of the components of the world economy, including markets, institutions, and policies.

Markets are one of the essential components of the world economy and are essential to the allocation of resources, the creation of wealth, and the distribution of goods and services. This chapter will explore the various types of markets, including stock markets, bond markets, and commodity markets, as well as the role of market competition in promoting economic growth and innovation.

Financial institutions, such as banks, play a crucial role in the world economy, as they facilitate the flow of capital between borrowers and lenders. This chapter will provide a detailed overview of the various types of financial institutions, including commercial banks, investment banks, and central banks, as well as their respective roles in the global financial landscape.

Economic policies, such as fiscal and monetary policies, are critical tools that policymakers use to promote economic stability and growth. Understanding how these policies work and their impact on the world economy is essential for individuals, businesses, and governments seeking to make informed decisions about the management of their finances and the regulation of the economy.

Part 3: Global Trade and International Agreements

Global trade is a fundamental component of the world economy and plays a critical role in driving economic growth, creating jobs, and promoting innovation. This chapter will provide a detailed overview of the history of global trade, the benefits and challenges of international trade, and the role of international trade agreements.

International trade agreements, such as the World Trade Organization (WTO) and the North American Free Trade

Agreement (NAFTA), are essential tools that promote international trade and economic growth. This chapter will provide a detailed overview of the various international trade agreements, their respective benefits and challenges, and the role they play in the world economy.

The benefits of international trade are numerous and include increased economic growth, job creation, and technological innovation. However, there are also challenges associated with international trade, including the risk of job displacement, wage stagnation, and environmental degradation. This chapter will explore these challenges in detail and provide insights into how they can be mitigated.

In conclusion, understanding the fundamentals of the world economy, the various components of the economic system, and the complexities of global.

Chapter 2: Understanding the Financial Landscape

Part 1: Overview of Financial Markets and Instruments

Financial markets play a crucial role in the functioning of the global economy. They are the primary mechanism through which individuals and institutions channel their savings and investments into productive uses. In this section, we will provide an overview of the financial markets and the instruments traded within them.

Financial markets can be broadly categorized into debt markets and equity markets. Debt markets are where debt instruments, such as bonds and notes, are traded. These markets allow governments, corporations, and other entities to raise capital by selling debt securities to investors. Equity markets, on the other hand, are where shares of stock in publicly traded companies are bought and sold. These markets enable companies to raise capital by selling ownership stakes to investors.

Within the debt and equity markets, there are a wide variety of instruments that can be traded. In the debt market, some of the most commonly traded instruments include Treasury bonds, corporate bonds, municipal bonds, and mortgage-backed securities. In the equity market, investors can buy and sell stocks in individual companies or invest in index funds, which track a broad range of stocks.

In addition to the debt and equity markets, there are also markets for commodities, currencies, and derivatives. Commodity markets allow investors to buy and sell physical goods such as gold, oil, and agricultural products. Currency markets enable investors to trade different currencies, such as US dollars, Euros, and Japanese yen. Derivatives markets allow investors to hedge against or speculate on movements in financial markets, by trading options, futures, and other derivatives.

Part 2: Understanding Stocks, Bonds, and Other Investment Vehicles

Stocks, bonds, and other investment vehicles are the primary tools investors use to allocate their capital in the financial markets. In this section, we will provide an overview of these instruments and the factors that influence their performance.

Stocks represent ownership in a company and are traded in equity markets. When investors buy a stock, they become a shareholder in the company and are entitled to a portion of its earnings and assets. The value of a stock is determined by factors such as the company's financial performance, the overall state of the economy, and investor sentiment.

Bonds are debt securities that are traded in debt markets. When an investor buys a bond, they are essentially lending money to the issuer of the bond, which could be a government, corporation, or other entity. The bond pays a fixed interest rate, known as a coupon, over a set period of time, and then returns the principal amount to the investor at maturity. The value of a bond is determined by factors such as the creditworthiness of the issuer, prevailing interest rates, and the length of the bond's maturity.

In addition to stocks and bonds, there are a wide variety of other investment vehicles available to investors. These include mutual funds, exchange-traded funds (ETFs), real estate investment trusts (REITs), and alternative investments such as private equity and hedge funds. Each of these vehicles has its own unique characteristics, risk profile, and potential for returns.

Part 3: Introduction to Banking and Financial Institutions

Banks and other financial institutions play a critical role in the functioning of the global financial system. They are the primary intermediaries between savers and borrowers, and provide a range of services to individuals, businesses, and governments. In this section, we will provide an overview of the different types of financial institutions and the services they offer.

Commercial banks are the most common type of financial institution. They provide a wide range of services, including checking and savings accounts, loans, and credit cards. Investment banks, on the other hand, specialize in underwriting and distributing securities such as stocks and bonds. They also provide advisory services to companies on mergers and a

Insurance companies are another important.

Chapter 3: Navigating the Complexities of Globalization

Part 1: Discussion of the impact of globalization on the world economy

Globalization has been a significant force shaping the world economy since the end of World War II. It refers to the increasing interconnectedness of economies and societies across the globe through the free flow of goods, services, capital, and ideas. The impact of globalization on the world economy has been both positive and negative. In this part, we will discuss the positive and negative effects of globalization on the world economy.

Positive effects of globalization on the world economy:

Increased economic growth: Globalization has increased economic growth by expanding trade, creating jobs, and increasing investment opportunities. As businesses expand their markets, they create new opportunities for themselves and for others.

Improved standard of living: Globalization has improved the standard of living in many parts of the world. As economies grow, they have more resources to invest in education, healthcare, and other social services. This has resulted in improved living conditions for people in many countries.

Greater access to information: Globalization has increased the access to information and knowledge. With the advent of the internet and other communication technologies, people have greater access to information about different countries and cultures, which has increased their understanding and appreciation of other cultures.

Negative effects of globalization on the world economy:

Unequal distribution of benefits: The benefits of globalization have not been evenly distributed. The rich have become richer, while the poor have become poorer. In many developing countries, globalization has led to a widening income gap between the rich and poor.

Job loss and economic insecurity: Globalization has led to job loss and economic insecurity in some countries. As companies relocate to countries with lower labor costs, many workers in developed countries have lost their jobs, while workers in developing countries may be subjected to poor working conditions and low wages.

Environmental degradation: Globalization has had a negative impact on the environment. The increased production and consumption of goods and services have led to higher levels of pollution and the depletion of natural resources.

Part 2: Analysis of the benefits and drawbacks of globalization

Globalization has both benefits and drawbacks. In this part, we will analyze the benefits and drawbacks of globalization.

Benefits of globalization:

Increased economic growth: Globalization has led to increased economic growth by creating new markets and expanding existing ones. This has resulted in increased trade and investment, leading to increased economic activity and job creation.

Improved standard of living: Globalization has led to an improved standard of living in many parts of the world. With the growth of the global economy, people have access to more goods and services, which has improved their living conditions.

Increased cultural exchange: Globalization has led to increased cultural exchange, which has increased understanding and appreciation of other cultures.

Drawbacks of globalization:

Unequal distribution of benefits: The benefits of globalization have not been evenly distributed. In many cases, the rich have become richer, while the poor have become poorer. This has led to a widening income gap between the rich and poor.

Job loss and economic insecurity: Globalization has led to job loss and economic insecurity in some countries. As companies relocate to countries with lower labor costs, many workers in developed countries have lost their jobs, while workers in developing countries may be subjected to poor working conditions and low wages.

Environmental degradation: Globalization has had a negative impact on the environment. The increased production and consumption of goods and services have led to higher levels of pollution and the depletion of natural resources.

Examination of the role of technology in globalization

Technology has played a significant role in driving globalization over the past few decades. With advancements in technology, the world has become more interconnected, leading to the creation of a global economy that transcends national borders. In this section, we will explore the various ways in which technology has impacted globalization.

Communication Technology:

The most obvious way technology has impacted globalization is through communication. With the internet and mobile technology, people can now communicate and collaborate with others from around the world in real-time. This has revolutionized the way businesses operate and has led to the creation of new business models. For instance, remote work has become more popular, allowing businesses to hire talented individuals from anywhere in the world.

In addition, communication technology has also made it easier for businesses to reach customers in other parts of the world. Companies can now use social media platforms and other online tools to market their products to a global audience. This has led to increased competition, but also increased opportunities for businesses to expand and grow.

Transportation Technology:

Transportation technology has also played a significant role in driving globalization. The development of faster, more efficient transportation methods has made it easier and more cost-effective to move goods and people across borders. This has led to increased trade and has made it easier for businesses to operate globally.

For example, the rise of air travel has made it possible for people to travel to other parts of the world in a matter of hours. This has led to increased tourism and has made it easier for businesses to conduct face-to-face meetings with clients and partners in other parts of the world.

Supply Chain Technology:

Advancements in supply chain technology have also had a significant impact on globalization. With the rise of e-commerce, businesses can now source goods and services from anywhere in the world. Supply chain technology has made it easier to track products and manage inventory, reducing costs and improving efficiency.

In addition, supply chain technology has made it easier for businesses to manage their operations globally. For instance, companies can now use cloud-based software to manage their supply chains from a central location, making it easier to coordinate activities across multiple locations.

Data and Information Technology:

Data and information technology have also played a critical role in globalization. With the rise of big data and artificial intelligence, businesses can now analyze vast amounts of data to gain insights into global markets and customer behavior. This has led to the creation of new business models and has enabled businesses to make more informed decisions.

Moreover, the development of block chain technology has made it easier and more secure to conduct global financial transactions.

This has reduced the need for intermediaries and has made it easier for businesses to operate globally.

Conclusion:

Technology has been a key driver of globalization over the past few decades, and its impact is likely to continue in the future. With further advancements in communication, transportation, supply chain, and information technology, businesses will be better equipped to operate globally and compete in the global marketplace. However, it is also important to note that technology has its limitations and drawbacks, and it is essential to balance the benefits of technology with the social and environmental impact it may have on our world.

Chapter 4: The State of the World Economy

As the world economy constantly evolves, it is essential to understand the current state and the trends that are shaping it. This chapter provides an overview of the current state of the world economy, an analysis of global economic trends, and a discussion of the economic impact of major world events.

Overview of the current state of the world economy:

The world economy has experienced significant changes over the past few years. As of 2021, the global economy is projected to grow by 5.5%, following a 3.5% contraction in 2020 due to the COVID-19 pandemic. The economic recovery is expected to be uneven across countries and sectors.

The United States and China are the two largest economies in the world, and their economic growth and policies have a significant impact on the rest of the world. In the US, the economy is showing signs of recovery, but the labor market remains weak. The Chinese economy continues to grow, but the country is facing challenges such as trade tensions with the US, an aging population, and environmental issues.

Analysis of global economic trends:

Several trends are shaping the global economy. One of the most significant trends is digitalization. The use of technology and automation is transforming the way businesses operate, and this trend is expected to continue. Another trend is the rise of emerging economies. Countries such as China, India, and Brazil are becoming increasingly important players in the world economy.

The COVID-19 pandemic has also accelerated existing trends, such as the shift towards e-commerce and remote work. The pandemic has had a significant impact on the world economy, and its effects will likely continue to be felt for years to come.

Discussion of the economic impact of major world events:

Several major world events have had a significant impact on the world economy. The 2008 financial crisis, for example, led to a global recession and a period of economic instability. More recently, the COVID-19 pandemic has had a significant impact on the world economy. The pandemic has caused a global recession, disrupted supply chains, and forced many businesses to close.

Trade tensions between the US and China have also had a significant impact on the world economy. The two countries are the largest economies in the world, and their trade relationship is crucial for global economic growth. The ongoing trade tensions have led to increased uncertainty and reduced global economic growth.

In conclusion, understanding the current state of the world economy, analyzing global economic trends, and discussing the economic impact of major world events are essential for making informed decisions about investments and economic policies.

Chapter 5: Managing Risk in the World Economy

Part 1: Explanation of Different Types of Financial Risk

Market Risk:

Market risk refers to the risk of loss caused by changes in market conditions such as price movements, volatility, and liquidity. Market risk can affect all types of investments, including equities, bonds, and derivatives. It is usually caused by macroeconomic events such as changes in interest rates, geopolitical events, and changes in consumer behavior. Investors and financial institutions often use hedging strategies such as diversification, options, and futures contracts to manage market risk.

Credit Risk:

Credit risk is the risk that a borrower will fail to repay their debt obligation. This type of risk is commonly associated with lending, investing in corporate bonds, and trading in credit derivatives. Credit risk can occur due to borrower default, bankruptcy, or other events that may prevent the borrower from fulfilling their debt obligations. Investors and financial institutions manage credit risk by conducting credit analysis to assess the borrower's ability to pay back the loan and by setting limits on the amount of credit they extend to borrowers.

Liquidity Risk:

Liquidity risk is the risk that an investor or financial institution will not be able to sell their investments quickly or at a fair price. Liquidity risk can arise from market volatility, changes in market conditions, or changes in investor sentiment. It is commonly associated with investments in real estate, private equity, and certain types of debt securities. Investors and financial institutions mitigate liquidity risk by diversifying their portfolios and maintaining sufficient cash reserves to cover any unexpected needs for liquidity.

Operational Risk:

Operational risk refers to the risk of loss caused by the failure of internal processes, systems, or human error. This type of risk can arise from a wide range of events, including cyber attacks, employee misconduct, and natural disasters. Operational risk can lead to reputational damage, financial losses, and regulatory violations. Investors and financial institutions manage operational risk by implementing strong internal controls, conducting regular audits, and ensuring adequate risk management systems and processes are in place.

Systemic Risk:

Systemic risk refers to the risk of a collapse of the financial system due to a failure of one or more financial institutions or other significant events. This type of risk can lead to a ripple effect throughout the economy, causing widespread financial instability and economic decline. The 2008 financial crisis is a prime example of systemic risk, as the failure of several major banks and the mortgage market led to a global economic downturn. Investors and financial institutions manage systemic risk by implementing strong regulatory frameworks, monitoring market developments closely, and diversifying their investments to reduce the impact of market downturns.

Part 2: Strategies for Mitigating Financial Risk

To implement these strategies effectively, investors and financial institutions need to carefully consider the risks involved, their financial goals and objectives, and their risk appetite. For example, diversification can be achieved through investing in a mix of assets, such as stocks, bonds, and real estate, or investing in different geographic regions. This approach helps to reduce the impact of market volatility on the overall portfolio, but it is not a guarantee against loss.

Hedging is another popular strategy that can be used to offset potential losses. For example, a company that is exposed to fluctuations in currency exchange rates may use currency hedging instruments to protect against potential losses. This approach involves taking positions in currencies that are expected to move in the opposite direction to the company's exposure, thereby reducing the impact of currency fluctuations.

Insurance is another risk management tool that can be used to protect against financial losses. Insurance policies can be purchased to cover a wide range of risks, including property damage, liability, and business interruption. By transferring the risk to an insurance company, investors and financial institutions can reduce their exposure to financial loss.

Finally, risk transfer involves transferring the risk to a third party, such as through the use of derivatives. Derivatives are financial contracts that derive their value from an underlying asset or index. For example, a futures contract is a derivative that allows the buyer to purchase an asset at a predetermined price at a future date. By using derivatives, investors and financial institutions can reduce their exposure to financial risks.

It is important to note that these strategies do not eliminate risk entirely, but rather help to manage and mitigate risk. Effective risk management requires careful analysis, planning, and execution, and should be tailored to the specific needs and objectives of the individual or organization. By using a combination of these risk management strategies, investors and financial institutions can protect themselves against financial losses and improve their overall portfolio performance.

Part 3: Real-World Examples of Financial Risk Management

One real-world example of financial risk management is the use of derivatives to hedge against market risk. For instance, a company might use futures contracts to lock in a price for a commodity that they will need in the future. This way, if the price of the commodity increases, the company will not be affected because they already have a contract in place at the agreed-upon price.

Another example is the use of insurance to mitigate credit risk. Credit insurance is a tool that can be used to transfer the risk of default to an insurance company. If a borrower defaults on a loan, the lender can file a claim with the insurance company to recover some or all of the losses.

Finally, diversification can be used to manage operational risk. For example, a company might have multiple suppliers for a key component of their product. If one supplier experiences a disruption, the company can still obtain the component from other suppliers, reducing the impact of the disruption on their operations.

In conclusion, financial risk management is an essential component of investing and financial decision-making. Understanding the different types of financial risks that exist, implementing effective risk management strategies, and learning from real-world examples are all critical to managing risk and protecting against potential losses.

Chapter 6: Charting a Course for the Future

Part 1: Examination of potential future economic trends

One of the key trends that could impact the world economy in the coming years is demographic change. As populations in many developed countries age, there will be a growing demand for healthcare, pensions, and other services that could strain government budgets. At the same time, emerging markets such as China and India are experiencing a demographic shift towards younger populations, which could drive economic growth and development.

Another important trend is technological advancement, which has the potential to transform many sectors of the global economy. For example, the rise of artificial intelligence and automation could disrupt traditional industries and change the nature of work. Similarly, advancements in renewable energy and transportation technology could transform the energy sector and reduce carbon emissions.

Environmental factors are also likely to play a significant role in the future of the world economy. Climate change, for example, could lead to more frequent and severe natural disasters, which could have significant economic impacts. The shift towards sustainable business practices and investments in clean energy could also create new economic opportunities and drive growth in certain sectors.

Finally, emerging markets are expected to play an increasingly important role in the global economy. As populations in these regions grow and become more affluent, there will be new opportunities for trade and investment. However, emerging markets also face significant challenges such as political instability, corruption, and inadequate infrastructure, which could impede their development.

Overall, understanding these potential future economic trends is crucial for businesses, investors, and policymakers to anticipate and prepare for the challenges and opportunities that lie ahead.

Part 2: Analysis of Potential Challenges Facing the World Economy

Rising income inequality is one of the major challenges facing the world economy. The gap between the rich and the poor has been widening in many countries, with wealth increasingly concentrated in the hands of a few. This trend has been driven by a variety of factors, including globalization, automation, and declining unionization rates. The rise of the gig economy and the prevalence of precarious work has also contributed to the problem, as workers struggle to secure stable, well-paying jobs. Income inequality not only has social and ethical implications, but it can also have a negative impact on economic growth, as the middle class, which is an engine of economic activity, shrinks.

Political instability is another major challenge facing the world economy. This can take many forms, including terrorism, civil war, and political polarization. In recent years, we have seen an increase in political polarization in many countries, with political discourse becoming more divisive and polarized. This can lead to a lack of consensus on economic policy, making it difficult to address key issues such as inequality, poverty, and unemployment. Political instability can also have a negative impact on investment, trade, and economic growth, as investors and businesses become hesitant to invest in countries with uncertain political environments.

Environmental degradation is another significant challenge facing the world economy. Climate change, deforestation, and pollution are just a few of the environmental issues that are threatening the global economy. These issues can have a negative impact on economic growth, as they can reduce productivity, increase the cost of doing business, and disrupt global supply chains. Climate change, in particular, has the potential to cause significant economic damage, as rising sea levels, extreme weather events, and crop failures could lead to significant economic losses.

Protectionist trade policies are also a potential challenge facing the world economy. In recent years, we have seen an increase in protectionist trade policies, such as tariffs and trade barriers. These policies can have a negative impact on global trade and investment, leading to reduced economic growth and increased volatility in financial markets. Protectionist trade policies can also exacerbate inequality, as they often benefit large corporations at the expense of smaller businesses and individuals.

Finally, geopolitical tensions and the ongoing threat of global pandemics are potential challenges facing the world economy. Geopolitical tensions, such as the ongoing tensions between the US and China, can lead to trade disruptions and increased volatility in financial markets. The ongoing threat of global pandemics, as demonstrated by the COVID-19 pandemic, can have a significant impact on the global economy, disrupting global supply chains, reducing demand, and causing economic downturns.

Overall, there are many potential challenges facing the world economy in the coming years. By understanding these challenges, policymakers, investors, and businesses can be better equipped to navigate an uncertain economic landscape and plan for the future.

Part 3: Discussion of Strategies for Addressing Future Economic Challenges

One important strategy for addressing future economic challenges is the promotion of sustainable development. As discussed in the previous section, environmental degradation is a significant challenge facing the world economy, and addressing this challenge will require a concerted effort to promote sustainable practices in areas such as energy production, transportation, and agriculture. Governments and international organizations can work to promote the adoption of renewable energy sources, encourage the development of green infrastructure, and implement policies that incentivize sustainable practices.

Another key strategy for addressing future economic challenges is the promotion of education and skill development. As technology and automation continue to transform the global economy, there is a growing need for workers to acquire new skills and knowledge to remain competitive in the job market. Governments and educational institutions can play a crucial role in promoting the development of new skills and knowledge, and in providing training and education programs that can help workers adapt to the changing economic landscape.

A third strategy for addressing future economic challenges is the promotion of international cooperation and collaboration. Global challenges such as climate change, financial instability, and pandemics require a coordinated international response, and governments and international organizations must work together to develop effective solutions. This can involve the sharing of information and expertise, the development of common policies and programs, and the promotion of international trade and investment.

In addition, innovation and technology will continue to play a key role in driving economic progress and addressing future challenges. Governments and private sector companies can work to promote research and development in areas such as artificial intelligence, robotics, and biotechnology, and to ensure that these advances are used in ways that promote economic growth and social welfare.

Finally, the promotion of greater economic and financial integration can help to address future economic challenges by promoting greater efficiency and reducing barriers to trade and investment. This can involve the development of regional economic blocs, the promotion of international financial cooperation, and the development of common regulatory frameworks.

In conclusion, there are many potential economic trends and challenges that could shape the future of the world economy. By understanding these trends and challenges, and by implementing effective strategies to address them, governments and international organizations can help to promote a more prosperous and sustainable global economy.

Conclusion:

In conclusion, the economic landscape is complex and ever-changing. The world economy is shaped by a wide range of factors, including technological advancements, demographic changes, and environmental factors. While there are many potential challenges on the horizon, there are also numerous opportunities for growth and progress. By understanding the fundamentals of the world economy, as well as the potential challenges and opportunities that lie ahead, readers can be better equipped to navigate an uncertain economic landscape and plan for the future. Through effective risk management and a focus on innovation and collaboration, we can work together to create a more stable, prosperous, and sustainable global economy.

www.ingramcontent.com/pod-product-compliance
Lightning Source LLC
Chambersburg PA
CBHW070319240526
45467CB00046B/2058